Trains

Emily Bone

Designed by Sam Chandler

Illustrated by Christyan Fox

Train expert: Anthony Coulls, Senior Curator,
National Railway Museum

Reading consultant: Alison Kelly, Principal Lecturer at Roehampton University

Contents

Train travel

Trains travel along railway tracks, taking people and all kinds of things from one place to another.

This train is carrying passengers across a desert in Namibia, Africa.

People carrier

Passenger trains carry people. They are made up of cars that are linked by couplers.

The engineer controls the train from the cab.

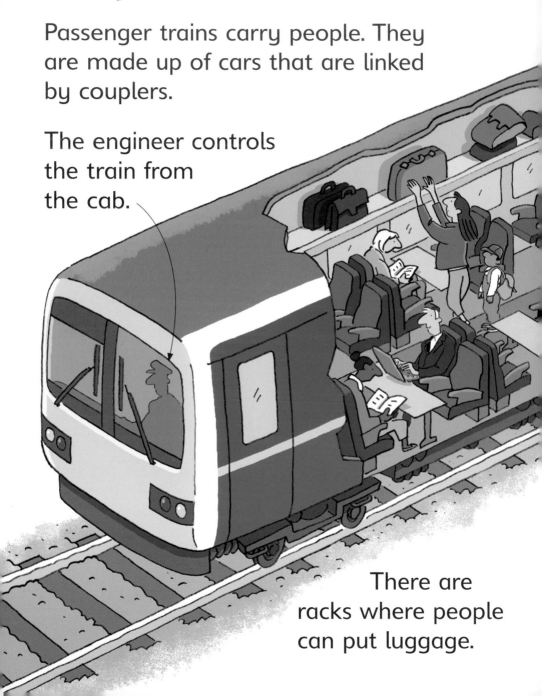

There are racks where people can put luggage.

This train has
two cars. They
are linked by a door.

Part of this train has been cut
away so that you can see inside.

In some countries, there are double-decker
trains that can carry twice as many people.

Moving goods

Freight trains pull freight cars that carry goods.

Large objects, such as vehicles, are loaded onto flat cars.

This train is pulling covered cars. They are sealed so the goods inside are kept safe and dry.

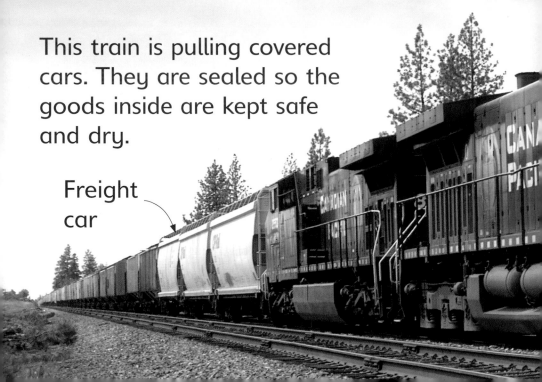

Freight car

Tank cars carry liquids or gases that are pumped in at the top.

Open cars are filled with heavy materials, such as stones, coal or sand.

Making tracks

A railway track is made up of two metal rails fastened to blocks, called ties.

Here, you can see lots of tracks leading into a station. The lights are signals that tell trains when it is safe to move.

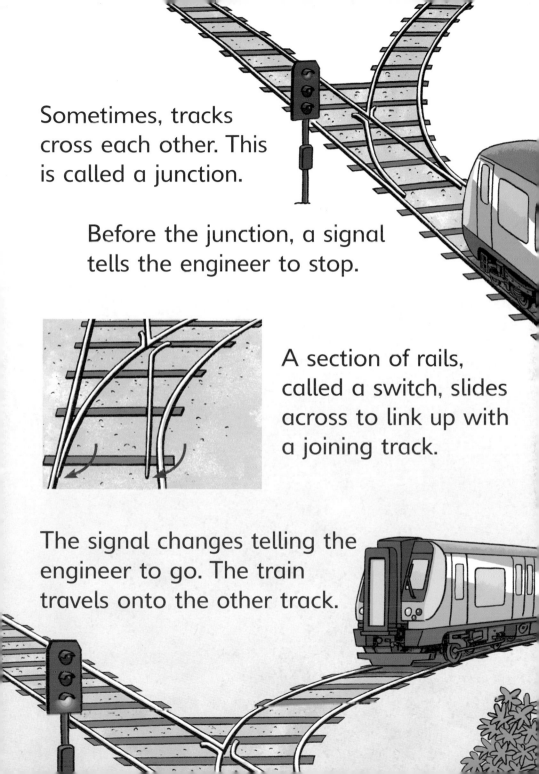

Sometimes, tracks cross each other. This is called a junction.

Before the junction, a signal tells the engineer to stop.

A section of rails, called a switch, slides across to link up with a joining track.

The signal changes telling the engineer to go. The train travels onto the other track.

Flat track

Bridges and tunnels make a flat route for trains across roads, water or mountains.

This train is crossing a bridge over a valley in Switzerland. It has just come out of a tunnel through the mountain.

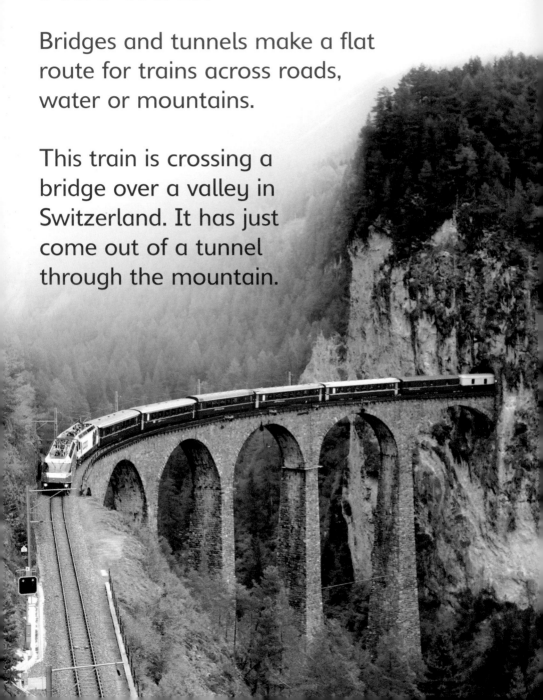

The longest bridge in the world is in China. It takes an hour for a train to cross it.

Railway tunnels are built using tunnel boring machines that cut into hills and mountains.

A sharp, spinning disc slices into the hill, making a hole.

Broken-up pieces of rock are carried away on a conveyor belt.

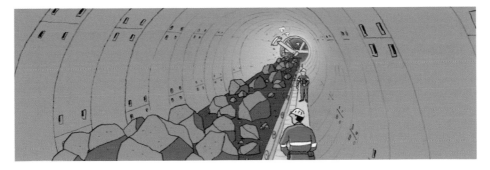

The machine moves along. Then, metal panels are fixed to the tunnel walls behind.

11

Driving a train

The engineer makes a train go forward or stop, and also changes its speed.

He presses buttons and levers in the cab to control the train.

This engineer is pushing the power handle, to make the train go forward.

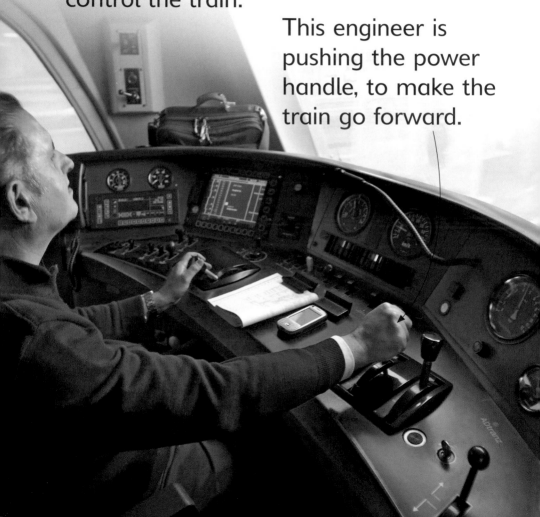

When the engineer stops the train, he presses a button to open the doors.

He leans out of the cab window to see if all the passengers have boarded.

A beeping noise in the cars warns passengers that the doors are closing.

A screen shows that all the doors have closed. Then, it is safe to go.

Train control

People in control rooms use computers to change railway signals, so trains travel along the right tracks.

The screen shows controllers the position of different trains.

Controllers make sure that problems are dealt with quickly and safely.

If a train breaks down, the engineer calls a controller to let him know.

The controller changes signals to make other trains in the area stop.

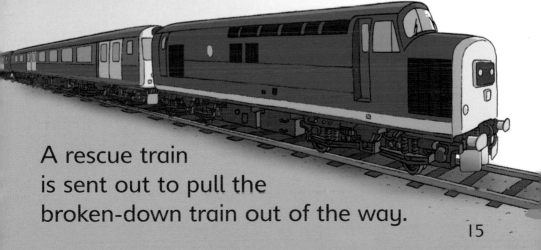

A rescue train is sent out to pull the broken-down train out of the way.

Running on steam

The first trains were built over 200 years ago. They had big engines, called steam engines.

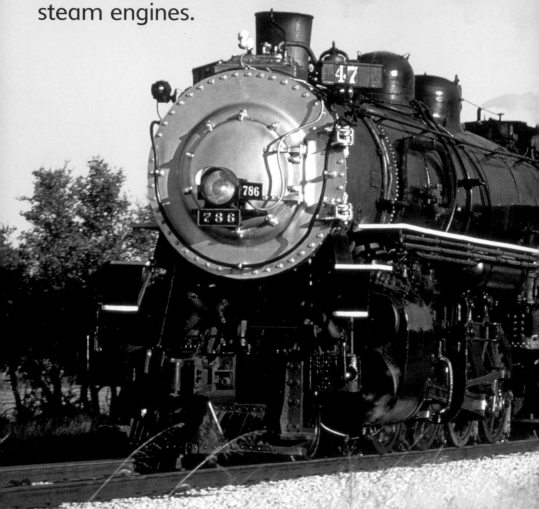

This train was built in the U.S.A. in 1916. It carried passengers across Texas.

Coal was burned to boil water and make steam. This powered the engine.

The engine turned sets of wheels under the train, pushing it along the track.

Passenger car

Some steam trains had metal bars on the front to push animals off the tracks.

Diesel engines

After steam engines, diesel engines were used to power trains.

This is a Streamliner train from the 1950s. The diesel engine is at the front of the train.

Diesel engines need diesel fuel to work.

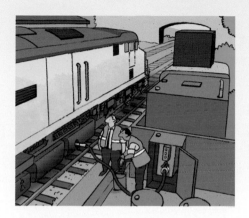

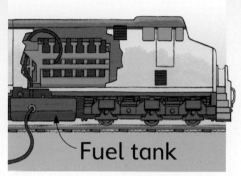

Fuel tank

A tank at the front of the train is pumped full of diesel fuel.

The diesel flows from the tank and into the engine, where it is burned.

The burning diesel provides the power to turn the train's wheels.

Electric trains

Electric trains pick up power as they move along.

This is a passenger train in Slovakia.

Pantograph

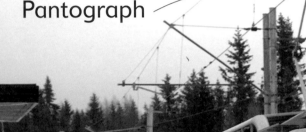

A metal arm, called a pantograph, gets electricity from the cables above the track.

Other electric trains are powered by an extra rail at the side of the main track.

Block

A metal block on the train presses down on the rail and slides along it.

Electricity travels from the rail, to the train. This powers the train.

If there is snow or ice on the rail, the block loses contact and the train stops.

In the city

Trains move people quickly around cities.

Monorail trains travel along a track above city streets, out of the way of traffic below.

This monorail is in Kuala Lumpur, Malaysia. It carries over a million passengers every day.

Some trains carry people underground, through tunnels.

Long escalators take people to and from the trains.

There are lots of overlapping tunnels under the streets, taking trains to different places.

Some trains don't have an engineer. They are controlled by a computer.

High-speed travel

High-speed trains are very fast electric trains that carry people quickly over long distances. They travel on separate tracks from other trains.

This high-speed train, called the JR500, goes to stations across Japan.

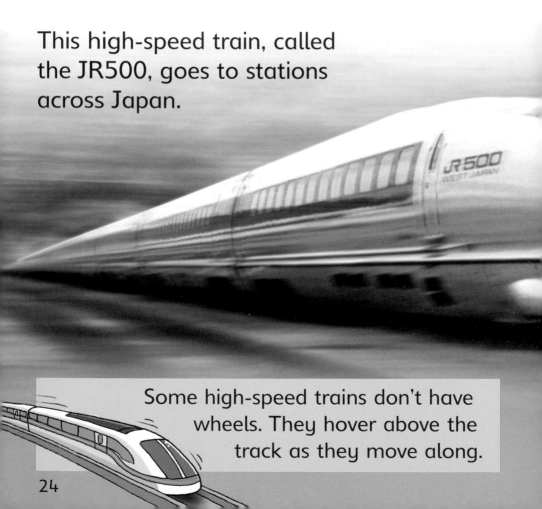

Some high-speed trains don't have wheels. They hover above the track as they move along.

Normal tracks have lots of bends. Trains have to slow down to go around them.

High-speed tracks are very straight, so trains on them can move faster.

This train's pointed nose helps it to cut through the wind.

Going up

Rack and pinion railways make it possible for trains to climb up steep slopes.

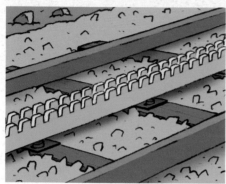

A grooved rail, called a rack, runs along the middle of the track.

There are grooved wheels, called pinions, on the underside of the train.

The pinions slot into the grooves in the rack. This stops the train from slipping back.

Funicular trains are pulled up and lowered down steep tracks by a cable.

The trains here take people from a beach to a cliff-top town in England. A cable is attached to the front of each train.

Going the distance

Sometimes, people travel on long train journeys that last for several days.

On some trains, passengers stay in rooms or cabins.

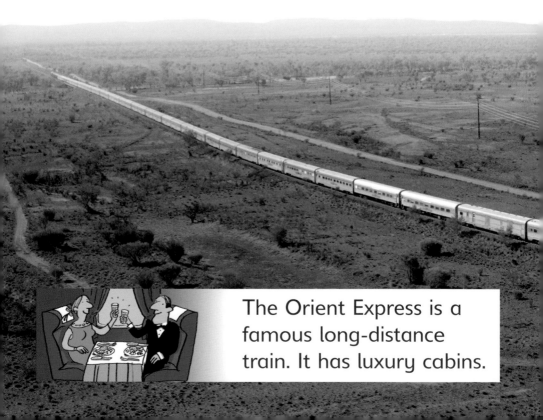

The Orient Express is a famous long-distance train. It has luxury cabins.

At night, beds are folded down from the cabin walls.

In the morning, a steward brings drinks and breakfast.

This is the Ghan train. It takes three days to travel across Australia.

Glossary

Here are some of the words in this book you might not know. This page tells you what they mean.

 car - the part of a train where passengers travel.

 cab - where the engineer sits to control a train.

 freight cars - trailers loaded with goods that are pulled by freight trains.

 ties - heavy blocks that hold the rails in a railway track in place.

 signals - lights by the side of the track that tell trains to go forward or stop.

 switches - sliding rails that allow a train to move from one track to another.

 pantograph - a metal arm that transfers power to an electric train.

Websites to visit

You can visit exciting websites to find out more about trains.

To visit these websites, go to the Usborne Quicklinks Website at **www.usborne-quicklinks.com** Read the internet safety guidelines, and then type the keywords "**beginners trains**".

The websites are regularly reviewed and the links in Usborne Quicklinks are updated. However, Usborne Publishing is not responsible, and does not accept liability, for the content or availability of any website other than its own. We recommend that children are supervised while on the internet.

This diesel train, called The Prospector, was built in Canada in 1941. It now takes tourists on short journeys.

Index

Acknowledgements

Photographic manipulation by John Russell
American Editor: Carrie Armstrong

Photo credits

The publishers are grateful to the following for permission to reproduce material:
cover © **age fotostock/SuperStock**; p1 © **Prisma/SuperStock**; p2-3 © **Photolibrary (Obert Obert)**;
p6-7 © **Animals Animals/Photolibrary (Phyllis Greenberg)**;
p8 © **Photolibrary**; p10 © **imagebroker.net/Photolibrary (Joachim E Rottgers)**;
p12 © **imagebroker.net/SuperStock**; p14 © **Siemens press picture**;
p16-17 © **Photolibrary (Ian Clark)**; p18 © **Bettmann/CORBIS**; p19 © **Transtock/SuperStock**;
p20 © **imagebroker.net/SuperStock**; p22 © **Prisma/SuperStock**;
p24-25 © **International News Sevice/Rail Photo Library**;
p27 © **Loop images/Photolibrary (Jason Friend)**; p28-29 © **David Hancock/Alamy**;
p31 © **Photolibrary (Chris Harris)**.

Every effort has been made to trace and acknowledge ownership of copyright. If any rights have
been omitted, the publishers offer to rectify this in any subsequent editions following notification.